JAPANESE EROTISM

JAPANESE EROTISM

Presented by
Bernard Soulié
Translated by Evelyn Rossiter

Crescent Books
New York

Most of the illustrations in this volume are reproduced with the kind permission of the University of Indiana, Bloomington, Indiana, (Institute for Sex Research), which also gave us valuable guidance for which we are most grateful.
The documents on pages 2, 5, 6, 7, 11, 18, 26, 27, 36, 37, 80, 81, 88, 90, 91, 94, 95 and 96 are from the Gichner Foundation, Washington. We wish to thank Mr. Lawrence E. Gichner for permission to use them.

Designed and produced by
Productions Liber SA

First English edition published by
Production Liber SA

I.S.B.N. 0-517-351153

This edition is distributed by Crescent Book
a division of Crown Publishers, Inc.

a   b   c   d   e   f   g   h

Printed by
Printer Industria Gráfica SA
Provenza, 388   Barcelone, Espagne
Depósito legal: B. 29637-1981
Printed in Spain

As radio cars and helicopters keep the crowd in order, an imposing procession of women follows a group of laughing priests, while expressionless police officers hold the onlookers back. This scene would be fairly commonplace were it not for the nature of the object in honor of which the procession is being held: the phallus. Finely sculpted specimens made of carefully polished wood are to be found in dozens of sanctuaries dedicated to the cult of Shinto, the ancient religion which preceded Buddhism and which still pervades Japan today.

Needless to say, in such a country there is no taboo on sexuality or sexual images. Sex has always been very much taken for granted. The place it occupies in literature and the arts is therefore not surprising. Graphic treatment of the subject in Japan has been abundant, of high quality and distinctly original, even when compared to the work of the Chinese masters.

Japanese erotic art blends refinement of line with a brutally realistic depiction of the sexual act. The attendant commentary, often expressed by the protagonists themselves, gives an unabashed account of intimate anatomical and physiological details, while the sexual organs, particularly that of the male, are shown as being vastly larger than life during and just before intercourse. In many instances, however, the rest of the protagonists' bodies is clothed, and sumptuously so. Their finery and hairstyle, as well as the decor of the scene, provide clues as to their social background. Certain pictures include accessories designed to enhance pleasure, whether

つおらや
めしようがにうきき
おまんまのまくに
おきんこそー
やうりう一久
テくイ〜をくくりすゝきも
えんかい〜がもあをせ

つレすらんあまれいてるらー
今おまんませんありせせると
思つくそのまく二一口に
おりつそくてしこ持てある
もて

solitary or shared, such as the harigata (artificial penis) or the higo-zuiki (ring hastening erection).

A salient feature of Japanese erotic art—and one which makes it all the more interesting—is the fact that the greatest illustrators, renowned for their talents as landscape or portrait artists, have always contributed to it.

Japanese erotism is inseparable from a familiar mythology which still means a great deal to an entire people. From the 5th century, when the principality established in the Yamato Plain (near Kyoto) first became predominant, right up till the recent past, all Japanese sovereigns were revered as being quite literally the descendants of Amaterasu, the goddess of the sun. The present emperor Hirohito was the first to break with this tradition when, in order to save his throne, he dropped his claim to such divine ancestry just after the defeat of Japan in 1945.

This exceptional historical continuity was aided by the continuity of the cult of Shinto. Having as its basis an intimate relationship between man and nature, it gave Japanese eroticism its particular strength. It occurs in as early a legend as that of the creation of the world. The splendid lance which penetrated the cesspool from which the first island emerged as a splash, is an unmistakable symbol—that of the primeval sexual act. Having driven into the belly of the world the giant penis which they had received from their celestial ancestors, Izanagi and Izanami then used it to come down to earth. Their weapon then became a tree of life, around

which they playfully revolved, in their various directions. When they eventually met, Izanagi imitated the lance and Izanami the earth which was opened by the magic stake, by making love together so as to engender other islands. Eventually, however, after numerous pregnancies, Izanami gave birth to the god of Fire and died, her sexual organs burnt by her last child.

Even if these and other legends remind us of some of the tales of Greek mythology, they differ at least in one way: the ever-present influence of their sexual content. For evidence of this one has only to travel through the Japanese countryside and come across two mating trees, standing on their freshly cut branches as if on legs: one of them has a penis, carved from another of its branches, specially chosen for the angle between it and the trunk. One even finds this everyday erotism occasionally in the art of pastry-making: there is particular kind of tasty cake made in the shape of an erect male penis on the point of ejaculation.

At a very early stage, Japanese civilization integrated erotism in everyday life. It was indulged freely in both courtly society and among the common people, who had access to a number of sexual manuals which were, in the real sense of the term, bedside reading. The art of the kiss, which had been codified as early as the 9th century, involved the coupling of the tongues of the two partners in an intimate embrace during copulation, or Sapphic games in which one of the protagonists used a harigata *instead of a penis. Stone sculptures depicting an intertwined couple, joined by both sex organs and mouths, can still be seen in the rural areas of Japan.*

 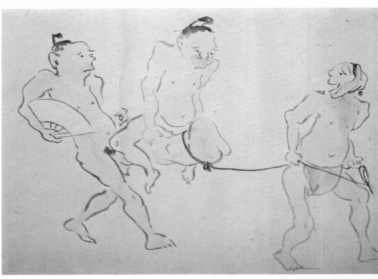

What we now call group sex was already being practised in Japan ten centuries ago. While the cathedrals of Europe were filled with a fear-stricken populace dreading the approach of the year 1000, both men and women thronged into the Shinto temples for the game of the great phallus. Those competing tried to excite each other and cause the erection of the penis. The male whose outstretched organ subsided last, despite the unceasing provocations of the opposing camp, was declared the winner. Two centuries earlier, Buddhism, which had come from India via China in 552, appropriated the erotism of the Shinto cult. Two sects advocated accession to the supreme wisdom through sexual union and associated asceticism with lust. The servants of the cult of Amaterasu, the goddess of the sun, did not wait for this foreign example in order to reconcile the absence of a female companion and the gratification of their sexual urges. The first syllable of their goddess's name could only heighten their enthusiasm, as ama means penis. Being unable to penetrate the Green Snake or pass through the Royal Door—two metaphors among many designating the opposite sex—they, like the Samurai, possessed their young disciples by the Path of the Ephebes, the jaku-dô.

 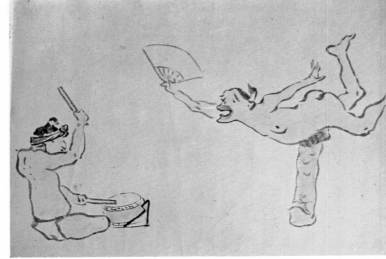

The preponderance of the phallus reached such a level that male homosexuality could not be viewed as a perversion. Writers often dwelt in detail on the careful preparations which accompanied such acts; Kumadori Shunjin, for example, added to his readers' excitement by changing the object of a Samurai's desire into a woman at the last moment, and then having the warrior die before being able to consummate the act, while having reconciled himself to the change in his partner.

As for the status of women, an author from the Muromachi period (1378 to 1573) observed that Japanese lords married only in order to secure possession of a splendid belly. However, those bellies could not have been headless, because in the 13th century one of them, named Jinko-Kotu, seized power and was followed in various periods by ten others. Sex quite literally carried them to the top. The emperor, even when married, used to keep concubines. Moreover, those of his children who were borne by his concubines, though brothers and sisters by blood, were authorized to have sexual relations provided that they were not of the same mother. Mothers and daughters clearly stood to gain a great deal from such an arrangement. It stimulated both their desire for power and the pleasure which they derived from the men—and for that matter, the women—who came and went in their beds.

In this way both history, and before it tradition and legend, often bore the stamp of a sexuality which pervaded the arts and literature and dominated life at court.

The Kabuki theatre soon provided artists with a new range of models. Thenceforth they were able to draw their inspiration from its portrayal of popular themes, its melodramatic subjects and, above all, the love-lives of transvestites. These had replaced women on stage, because of the ban on female performers, and they continued to wear the clothes and hairstyles of women even in town.

The 18th century was approaching, and with it the golden age of Japanese erotic art.

Two names dominate the period: Utamaro and Hokusaï. In the chronology of Japan their work falls within the second half of the reign of the Tokugawa, who governed the country from 1615 to 1867, or more than two hundred and fifty years, and made Edo, now Tokyo, their capital.

The Western world did not discover Utamaro and Hokusaï until long after their deaths. And it did so quite by chance. An imperial official who was in Paris to prepare the Japanese pavilion at the 1878 Universal Exposition happened to show The Twelve Hours of the Green Houses, the Song of the Pillow, illustrated by Utamaro, and Young Pine Shoots, the work of Hokusaï, to the French writer Edmond de Goncourt (who later founded the famous literary prize).

Goncourt compared the drawing of a penis in the last of these works to the hand which is thought to be the work of Michelangelo, now in the Louvre. Elsewhere he writes lyrically of "the fury of these copulations, as if transported by rage", the "animal frenzies of the flesh" and the "devouring kisses of mouth upon mouth". His friend Rosny Jeune, who was also highly impressed, emphasized "the countless affinities between art and erotism" and used the phrase "garden of delights" to describe those Green Houses which were the homes of courtesans richly versed in the fine arts and literature.

Besides Utamaro and his school and Hokusaï (who had two of his daughters among his disciples), this volume also honors many others masters of Japanese erotic art, including Toyokuni, Kusinada, Shunsho, Eisen and their successors, who are its most brilliant representatives.

AN UNUSUAL HERO OF THE EROTIC SAGA: THE BONZE.

Although the bonzes were forbidden to engage in any sort of sexual relations, chastity seems to have been the exception rather than the rule in most of their communities. The superiors of the monasteries used to keep their favorites, while their subordinates were content to initiate their young disciples into homosexuality. Even so, women were no rarity in the temples. They were appointed on the basis of a contract concluded for several months, or even years. They then had a chance of becoming the concubine of a high-ranking bonze: a sort of governess, in a position to enjoy the offerings in cash and kind made by the faithful. On the other hand they were more often than not doomed to the life of a recluse, a constant prey to the sexual appetites of their masters.

These Japanese nuns soon came to be known as Madame Daikoku, as they were relegated to the altar of a god of good luck which bore that name and which was usually located in the kitchen, to keep them out of sight of the visitors. Ihara Saikaku described their existence in a novel published in 1686. His heroine, in her quest for a new protector, managed to get herself taken on by resorting to a subterfuge which was then quite common among courtesans. She entered the temple disguised as a boy, her head shaved down the middle, in the manner of the favorite. An armed manservant accompanied her, to increase her chances of success, and presented the young woman as a ronin, or Samuraï looking for a lord who might be prepared to include him among his troops, and anxious to take advantage of his freedom in order to share for a while the entertainments of the monks.

The trick having succeeded, the young woman became the concubine of a superior of the monastery and stayed with him for several months. When she got tired she used another ploy to escape: she pretended to be pregnant.

The extreme fondness of the bonzes for sex has enlivened many a tale. Their sexual exploits, especially in the light of the rule of chastity which they were supposed to abide by, made them

the heroes of legendary stories which were enlarged on with the passage of time by oral tradition and also by the erotic literature, in some cases illustrated. This was the case with *Fulkuro Zoshi-é Kotoba*, who related the adventures of a bonze whose sexual prowess made him the plaything of countless partners, once he had yielded to the whims of a great lady whose husband had died.

In this respect a word is in order about the role played by widows, of all ages, in Japanese erotica. They are usually protrayed as being consoled quite soon after their husband's death by a new spouse or lover whom they compare favorably to the deceased (see, in this book, one of the subjects dealt with by the school of Utamaro). When she has not yet made up her mind she is shown as consumed by impatience—further heightened by desire—as she unrelentingly searches for a partner capable of bringing her to orgasm (see also *Tsumagazane*, by Bizanjin).

In addition to the rich widow, to whom ladies-in-waiting one day bring the heroic monk of *Fukuro Zoshi-é Kotoba*, a figure who appears perhaps less frequently in this sort of story is that of the nun who loses her virginity with him.

The tale which follows is an adaptation of *Fukuro Zoshi-é Kotoba* developed from the treatment of the theme by Tanadori in the early 17th century and later copied on many occasions. It is interesting to note that the story went the rounds at a time when the shogun régime was persecuting some 300,000 Japanese who had been converted to Christianity by Spanish and Portuguese missionaries, the first of whom had landed at Kyushu nearly a century before; many of the converts were even killed. Through the sexual behavior of the bonze, as related in this truculent tale, one catches a glimpse of the clash between Eastern and Western ways which reflects the difference between the two civilizations.

This illustration and the one on page 14 are taken from an early novel. In the first episode, a lord named Yosizane discovers a superbly beautiful woman among the prisoners brought back by his soldiers. He is enchanted by her and has a dream in which he has pardoned her with a view to seducing her. However, while he is asking her to join him in bed, his subaltern wakes him up to announce that she is about to be sentenced.

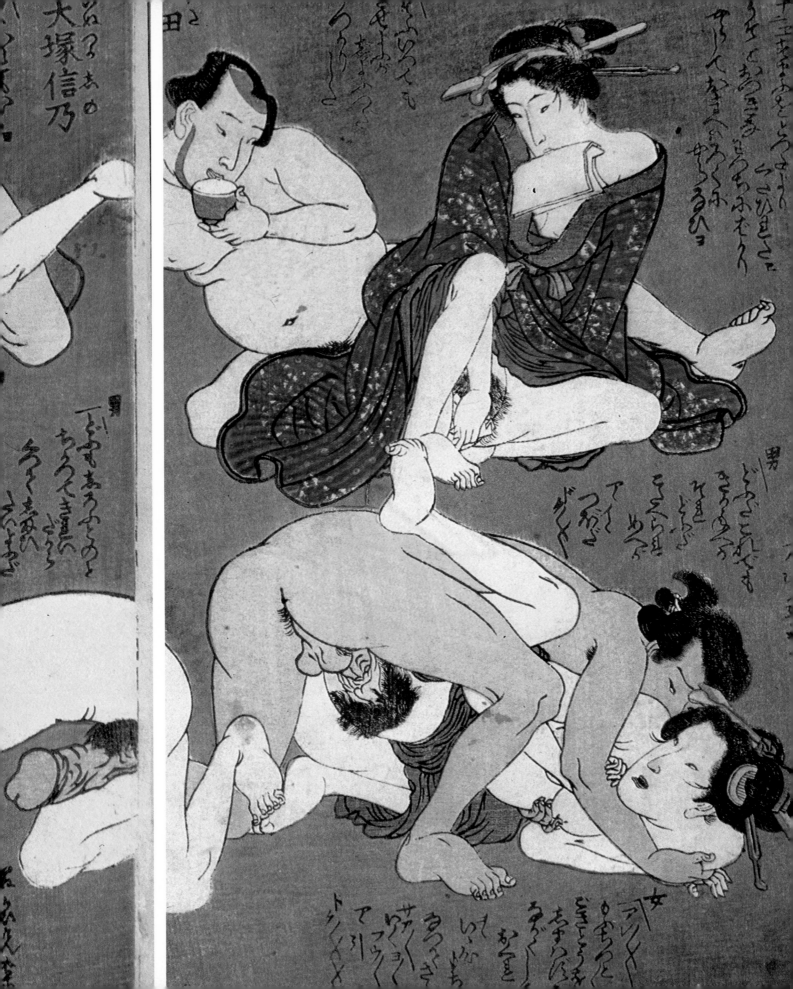

THE FERRYMAN WITH THE BURNING PHALLUS.

There are some shipwrecks which are caused neither by the fury of the river nor the clumsiness of the sailor, says an old proverb.

This notion is nicely illustrated by the adventures which befell a certain bonze who, rather than deriving his subsistence from contemplation, had become a ferryman. His choice of this occupation, while due to his marked fondness for inland navigation, also enabled him to sustain, through regular exercise, his remarkable sexual capacities.

Leaving the practice of the *jaku-dô,* or Path of the Ephebes, to his cloistered brothers, he favored assiduous frequentation of the *dan-bô,* the Princess of the Flowers, in other words the Royal Door, which opens at the approach of a respectably sized phallus at the peak of its glory. His was capable of excelling itself, and word spread quickly throughout the region.

One day the three waiting maids of a widowed chatelaine who lived nearby decided to find out for themselves whether the holy man's flattering reputation was genuine. They took it in turns to copulate with him as soon as the boat had pulled away from the shore. One after another they were able to savor the thrills provided by an apparently tireless partner. His phallus, which was of exceptional magnitude, showed no signs of wilting and enabled each one of them, time after time, to reach ecstasy.

When they got to the other side, seeing that the bonze was still fresh and willing, they invited him to go with them to meet their mistress, so that she too should feel the supreme pleasure which had been theirs. Since they could not bring their companion openly into the part of the castle which was supposed to be out of bounds for men, and where they lived together with their lady, they put him in a large bag, so that nobody would see him.

The lady of the house, touched by the sollicitude of her maids, promptly put the virility of her new boarder to the test. And he did not disappoint her, such was the ardor with which he led her through the forests of pleasure which he watered with his abundant sperm, while the soft juicy sap surging up from the innermost depths of the opening penetrated by his magnificent organ crowned it with the royal diadem of shared pleasure.

Left: the continuation of the previous episode: the beautiful captive is sentenced to death against the wishes of the lords, who have done their utmost to save her. She dies cursing Yosizane, who is shortly afterwards captured by a cruel prince. Yosizane then promises his daughter to his dog, as long as it brings back his enemy's head. His mission successfully completed, the animal takes the young girl off to the mountains, but she refused to make love with it. Her opposition continues until the day when a stranger, who claims to be under a spell, advises the girl to yield. When she eventually offers her body to the animal, it suddenly changes into a handsome young man who seduces her and leads her to a state of ecstasy.

Below: this engraving is one of the illustrations from an early novel, *Koi no Yatsu Fuji*. In fact it relates the subsequent adventures of the irrepressible Yosizane. After escaping, he goes off to find his daughter. Discovering her in ecstasy while making love with her dog, he feels his own lust mounting within him, knocks over the women of his retinue and reaches orgasm with two of them at the same time. However, his daughter's rejected fiancé, having surprised her in the company of her dog-lover, kills him.

So they made love all night without ever having to consult the rules of the forty-eight positions, as prescribed in the Pillow Book of Yoshiwara, the bedside book of the courtesans of Edo. The spring grass which covered with its silken mantle the golden triangle half hidden between the pink marble thighs of the young chatelaine were still shivering from the thrusts of her companion's milky phallus when dawn broke. Having enjoyed his favors unceasingly, she sent for her three maids and, on the pretext of thanking them for bringing her unspeakable joy, yielded her lover to them.

The three girls, barely able to restrain their desire, took the wondrous bonze off to the castle kitchens so as to feed him properly, and thereby ensure that, while not drinking or eating to excess, he would keep his incredible powers at their previous level. The appetites of their sex-craving bellies were already stimulating their sexual taste buds, which were swollen with impatient secretions. The man ate his meal, content with a pleasant interlude which did not exclude the expert caresses of his three friends. When he had finished eating, after what was for them an unconscionably long time, he took the oldest of them, and, without slackening his pace, displayed even greater ardor than he had on the boat, and a consummate mastery of the progressions of pleasure. The two others encouraged him, while surrounding him with every attention, so as to be better ready to take over from their elder companion. Then, while she was approaching orgasm, they made frenzied love with each other, their moans echoing those of the other couple.

"My lover's penis was like an outstretched pole;
I grasped it before falling".

Left: a Samurai, overwhelmed by the beauty of a boy, tries to seduce him. Later on the young man turns out to be a woman. Yet while the warrior, delighted with this transformation, prepares to pay tribute to the inviting sexual organ of his partner, he is killed, pierced by the dagger of an old man determined to avenge his sister's honor (from the same novel as the preceding plate).

Above: illustration from the novel *Koi no Yatsu Fuji,* third volume. A number of officers are raping a large group of women, until a servant of the house kills them one by one. He does so, however, the better to quench his own desire and allow them all, including his mistress, to savor an extreme pleasure. A widow who relishes the joys of sex greets a handsome young man who is thought to possess the finest aphrodisiacs. She allows herself to be led into his bedroom, eager to taste the magic drug. Then, disappointed in the effects of the potion, she throws the liar out and leaves him at the mercy of the first of her servants, who does with him as she pleases.

Above: 17th century print.
Below and right: two scenes from a roll containing twelve, describing various types of heterosexual behavior. Modern period.

Above and right, two scenes of heterosexual rape. These are paintings on paper, probably copies of late-19th century works taken from a roll which, on its wooden box, bears the lyrical title Spring Festival under the Trees.

At the peak of their pleasure, the tangle of bodies was such that it was impossible to tell who was making love to whom and how. Meanwhile, the chatelaine, her eye glued to the keyhole of the kitchen door, unknown to them, also enjoyed herself until evening.

And it was exactly as she had expected. Until the following morning, the monk thrust into her on her bed, while, next to them, her three maids writhed in excitement, inventing a thousand intimate caresses, aided by the judicious use of a double *harigata* which simultaneously relieved, in two of them, the absence of a penis.

Next morning there was a knock at the castle door. It was the sister of the lady of the house, who had come to pay her an unexpected visit. She was a nun in a nearby convent, and virgin. The two women spent the morning chattering.

When night fell the young nun had learnt from her sister the wonderful secret. Excited by glowing accounts of the monk's prowess she asked her sister for permission to savor, at long last, the joys of sex. And it was promptly granted. After she had experienced bliss several times with him alone or with the kind participation of the four women, who were delighted to initiate her into the heavenly pleasures of intercourse, she expressed another wish: to have her sisters in religion also share in her joys.

After one more day, in which only the bonze with the indefatigable penis took time off for physical nourishment, to sustain the strength he needed for the prodigious efforts he was expected to make, he was once more closed up in his bag. Rowing together instead of him,

the four women reached the opposite bank and then the convent.

When he was let out he found himself promptly the darling of the nuns, who were in sexual paroxysms on discovering pleasures hitherto unknown to them; he then rose to the summit of his power, offering his ever-ready phallus to the insatiable vaginas of the nuns. In a matter of days their education was complete. They had become skilled courtesans. To liven up their game even further and to give it the appearance of a divine mystery, they hit upon the idea of shutting up the man who had been satisfying them so unrelentingly in his bag, having first cut a hole big enough for his penis to protrude when required.

Moons followed moons, and summer followed spring, but the chatelaine, her three maids, her younger sister and the nuns of the convent never slackened their pace. Every day, every night they invented new games, and the ever fuller pleasures which they derived from them enabled them to slake their overpowering lust as they waited their turn to thrust into themselves the magnificent penis of the sole male member of the community.

Perhaps it was the lack of rest, or the uniquely cloistered state in which he—or most of him —was kept: none of those who learnt and revealed the extraordinary adventure which befell the ferryman could ever explain it clearly. But the fact is that his strength slowly declined, though he was well fed at all times.

Eventually along came the sad day when, having sown his last seeds, the bonze went back to his boat.

Later on his health recovered. But, doubtless considering that he had been satisfied more fully than large numbers of men with ardor equal to his, he was content thereafter to busy himself quietly with his work as a ferryman. And he became a part of legend.

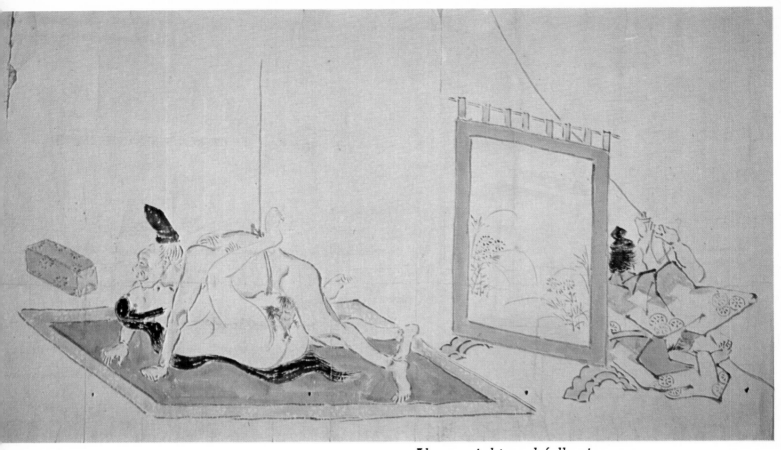

Above, right and following pages: four humorous watercolors, possibly copies of works by Mitsunobu, an artist of the late 19th century.

EROTISM AND MYTHOLOGY

The legend of Ama-no-Uzume belongs to Japanese mythology. In fact it is part of the great mystery of the creation of the world to which each culture has claimed to have the key. This legend led to the emergence of the cult of Shinto which is still deeply rooted in the Japanese soul. Sex is omnipresent in a cosmic tradition, the first known manifestations of which, on the archeological evidence, date from the neolithic period. A huge male organ suddenly thrust out of heaven and brought into being the original island where the Japanese Adam and Eve then proceeded to procreate a whole archipelago, in a burst of ardor which involved, for better but more often for worse, various gods, goddesses and fantastic creatures. This spectacle, which was sometimes terrifying and at other times burlesque, was witnessed by an attentive public: the gnomes and goblins of the sky who were to be become the household gods who, in the mind of a people still imbued with Shintoism, and despite the influence of Buddhism, possess numerous supernatural powers related to the ordinary gestures of everyday life.
At the pinnacle of this celestial empire, which was deliberately anthropomorphic in nature, stood the sun goddess, Amaterasu, of whom, we should not forget, the present Emperor Hirohito was thought to be the direct descendant, both literally and legally, at least until the defeat of 1945.

22

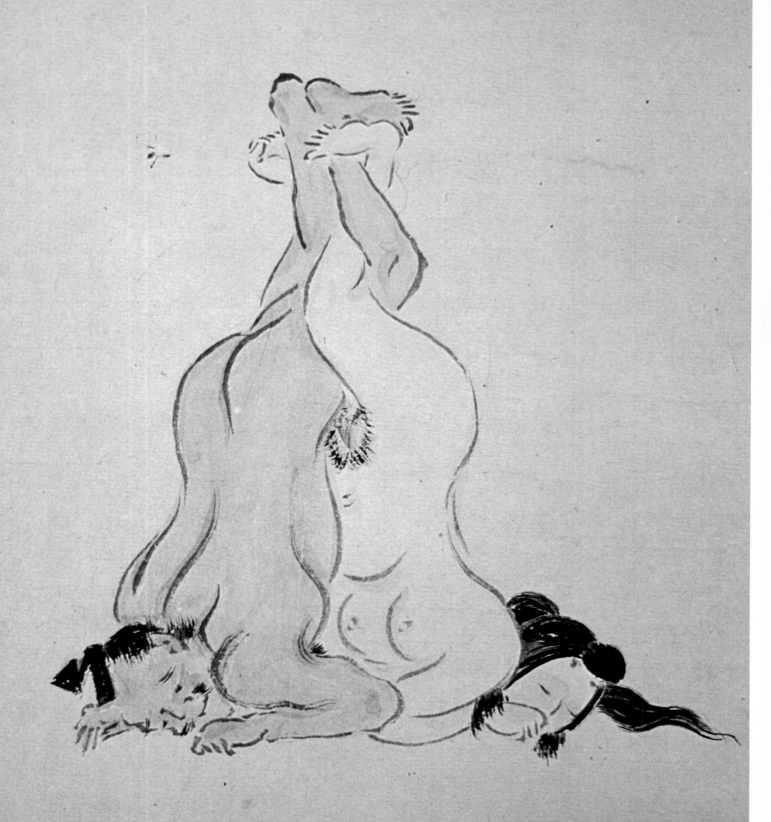

*"While awaiting the seed, woman is like the earth,
She likes to be turned over".*

Ama-no-Uzume is in a sense the negative of Amaterasu. She is the female of the heavens who is always ready to fornicate—as it were, the chief of the courtesans, endowed with special skills. Théo Lesoualc'h, a keen observer of Japanese customs and eroticism, and an authority on the subject, has drawn attention to the extraordinary intensity of the shows which are put on in certain special night-clubs and which far exceeds anything to be seen in the West.

Besides an early story contained in a collection published in the 8th century, the legend of Ama-no-Uzume has inspired a vast body of literature, some of which, duly toned down for use in schools, is still published.

The version presented here, which is for adult consumption, comes from the oral tradition, which was constantly enriched by the popular imagination with a myriad juicy details which testify to the Japanese fondness for mythological wonders as well as their sharp sense of humor.

THE NIGHT OF AMA-NO-UZUME

A goddess named Ama-no-Uzume was famous for her extreme attachment to the pleasures of the senses.

One day, or rather one night as the whole Earth had suddenly been plunged into darkness, the *kami* appealed to her.

Ama-no-Uzume hesitated. The *kami* were merely low-ranking and irreverent genies whose favorite pastime was to play pranks in poor taste on both gods and men. She therefore did

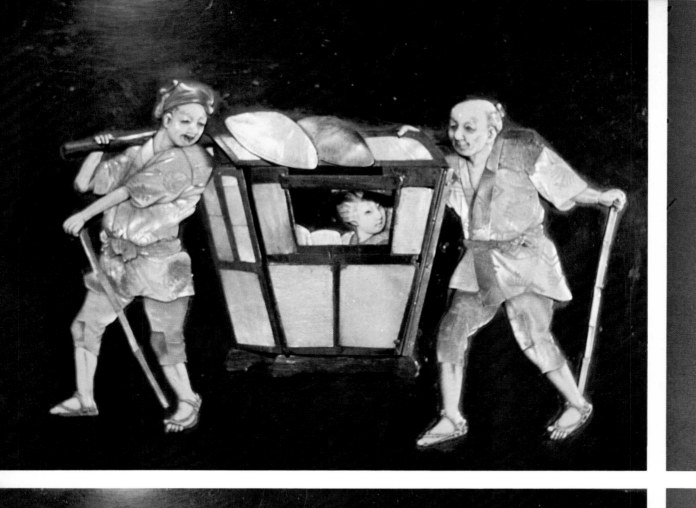

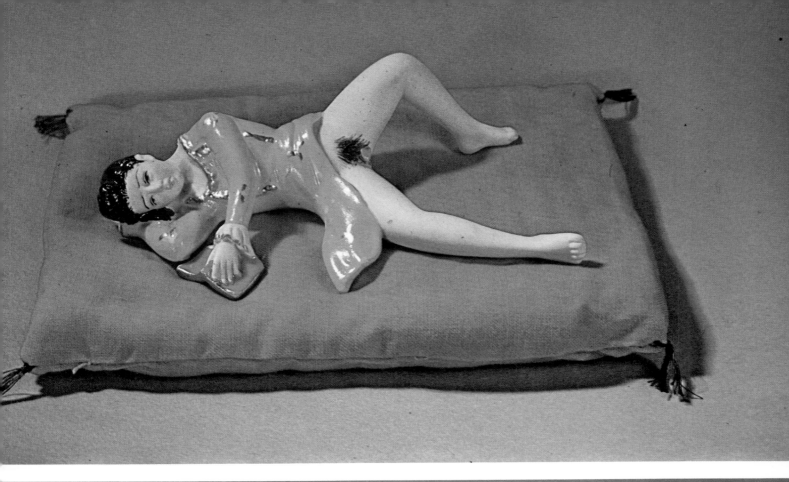

not readily agree to hear what they had to say. Perhaps they would secure for her some opportunity to quench the sexual appetite which goaded her by discovering some new form of physical enjoyment. Her curiosity aroused, she listened to them attentively, her eyes glistening, her mouth moist, her breasts suddenly stiffening and outstretched, her vagina already partially open, as she dreamt of a thousand orgasms commensurate with her reputation as an insatiable woman.

What the gnomes of the heavens did say was a surprise to her. They begged her to return to them the sun, which Amaterasu had confiscated by locking herself up with it in a cave and then blocking off the entrance with a huge boulder. The sun goddess thus intended to avenge the loss of one of her maids, whose brother, Suzano-wo, had caused her death.

Flattered to find herself entrusted with such an important mission, and secretly delighted at an opportunity to satisfy her jealousy towards Amaterasu by forcing her to yield, she adorned herself with flowers, and then, clad in her finest attire, began to dance, tapping out the rhythm of her steps with a lance against the ground. This curious ballet gradually grew faster, and she soon lost consciousness, abandoning herself utterly to the drunken hysteria of her own body which writhed in spasms of solitary pleasure as she now found herself separated from the recluse only by the boulder. As the moment of ecstasy approached, Ama-no-Uzume slowly undid her tunic. For an instant her triumphant breasts restrained her; then, arching her torso, she exposed them with a lascivious gesture, pointing them skyward. Like a jungle creeper her body, which was soon stripped to the belly, burst forth revealing her sexual organ, swollen with the juices of love as if, one moment later, some divine penis were to come out of the night and penetrate her.

As one might imagine, the *kami* had followed with growing interest this fascinating lesson in erotism. Yet, when it was over, their fondness for jest prevailed over their excitement, and they all burst out laughing; they were pleased because, thanks to Ama-no-Uzume, they had combined utility with the delight of the spectacle which her unbridled sensuality had offered them. Indeed they might even have lost sight of the purpose of this display, if Amaterasu, anxious to discover the cause of such commotion, had not ventured to glance out of her cave. Ama-no-Uzume, having recovered her composure, exploited her carelessness and told her rival that henceforth she had been replaced by a goddess whose beauty had captivated delighted her subjects.

Whereupon a crafty *kami* placed several feet away from Amaterasu a mirror in which she saw the face of a supremely beautiful woman whom she, in her emotional state, thought was the new Queen of the Heavens. This was too much for the proud goddess, and she strode impetuously out of her cave. As she did so the sun came back, and its splendid brilliance once more illuminated the universe.

This was how Ama-no-Uzume became the well-beloved goddess of the courtesans who, like her, were skilled at revealing their bodies to the greatest effect as night approached, behind the bamboo blinds of the Green Houses, as a prelude to the pleasure which they excelled at offering to their lovers.

28

The Island of Women (on this page and pages 28 to 35).
The island is one day invaded by the crew of a ship which has run aground. The queen chooses the sailor with the longest penis while her subjects share his companions. Then follows an orgy which, after the torrent of pleasure, leaves the sailors exhausted. In the morning they flee to the wreck of their ship, pursued by the women, who then, to their great dismay, find themselves alone.

"Each woman has two hearts.
Rather choose the lower one in which to plant your dagger".

"Even if she has left her door ajar
Make sure that your key is not rusty".

"Young virgins have moist sex organs and dry mouths
Whereas with old maids it is exactly the opposite".

"Unlike the lumberjack who chops them down.
A wordly woman will long be able to use
The resin which oozes from the pines".

"Never forget your sword on the battlefield,
The bravest warrior only has one".

"For the girl attendants at the public baths of Yoshiwara
All men have three legs".

"Among the sheaths abandoned by the vanquished,
The winner will be able to find all those
Which are well suited to his sabre".

"One can tell an experienced courtesan by her ability to distil pleasure
With as much care as others distil rice alcohol".

"The deep waters of the lake embroidered by the shadow of the ferns
Often bring more joy to fishermen
Than the well-stocked stream of youth".

"Choose the woman whose hands speak
Rather than the one who speaks with her hands".

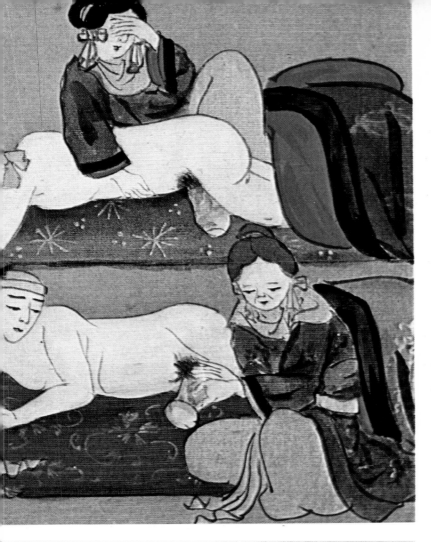

"If the cup is deep,
Plunge your tongue into it several times".

"An oil-soaked wick is not the only thing
Which burns at both ends".

"Rather than my husband's cow's milk,
I would sooner have that of the man
Who awaits me in the stable".

"Prefer the running water of the lake
To the stagnant water of the pond
As a place to sink your line".

"There is no one season
For sowing seed
On the plains of joy".

"Even with one's belly as full as an egg
And one's phallus as taut as a bow,
One can die both of love and hunger".

Reproductions of scenes from a roll of silk paintings done by hand (beginning of the century).

THE GEISHA, OR THE SUBLIMATION OF EROTISM

The geisha occupies a special place in the symbolism of Japanese erotism. She is, in a sense, its quintessence, although she is required to entertain men's minds without satisfying their sexual desires. For the most part this seems paradoxical only to a Westerner, who could readily tend to view this archetype of the female object as an invitation to savor the pleasures of the flesh which, in this case, could harldy be less refined than the exquisite ritual of the tea ceremony conducted for his sole benefit by this dream-like creature.

However, any sexual advances which he might contemplate would best be forgotten. With few exceptions, the geisha of today, like her predecessors, is not venal. She belongs to a guild which flourished during the Heian period, in about the year 1000, altough some historians date its formation some three centuries earlier, in the Nara Period (named after a town on the island of Honshu).

Many years later, when the shoguns made Edo their capital, the geishas were to be found at Yoshiwara. There they lived in an area which, though a part of the town of pleasure, contained no courtesans. Their presence, which could be construed as a sort of official

Above and right: scenes of heterosexual love painted, in the style of the 17th and 18th centuries, in eight colors on silk speckled with gold. The lovers are nobles.

approval for the place, certainly played a part in what can only be called the cultural ascension of this prominent center of eroticism.

The geisha learnt her craft from an early age. The candidate, who was presented by her parents, had barely reached the age of ten. She learned to make up her face a creamy white, which enhanced the vermilion brilliance of her lips and set off the black of eyebrows and eyelashes. Her throat and neck were also white, down as far as the beginning of the shoulders. She was given a sumptuous kimono, girdled by a broad *obi* knotted at the back, where it was adorned with a sort of thin silk cushion.

Next came the lessons in posture, which account for the traditionally graceful carriage of the geisha, in her characteristic wooden clogs, or *geta*. At the same time she acquired the skills of the perfect hostess, careful to meet her guest's wishes while taking account of his social position. She did all these things effortlessly, through the artistic and literary education which she had received. She became familiar with the latest novels soon after they appeared and also knew the biography of their authors; besides which she had mastered the art of *ikebana*, or the making of bouquets of flowers. She appreciated traditional music and was herself an excellent musician, entertaining her guests on the *shamisen*, a stringed instrument whose long neck makes it look like the sitar. She could also dance.

When she was ready to apply her craft she had to find her first employer, always a man.

His role was purely commercial, offering the young geisha a suitable framework for her advancement, the speed of which was likely to be influenced by the wealth and generosity of the visitors who frequented his establishment. Moreover the geisha did not remain imprisoned in the house; she was paid regular wages or allowed to work for hire in other houses.

In this way, as she mingled with the society of her day, it was not unusual for her to find a husband who would take pride in displaying his good taste and as well as the size of his income, in a world where it was measured by the number of women he could support. Whether as a concubine or merely as an occasional hostess, the geisha proved to be the best negotiator in the settlement of political or professional disputes between a husband or client and his competitors. She arranged meetings which, thanks to her charm, her knowledge and her pleasing way with people were very likely to be a success.

The value of a national institution can be measured by its longevity. This particular one has withstood all the upheavals which have occurred in the history of Japan.

Even though they do not begin their apprenticeship nowadays until the age of 16, the geishas still serve the Japanese economy with the same talent by contributing, in particular, to the success of public relations operations conducted both at home and abroad by the major corporations, which employ them as hostesses. While suspicion of engaging in prostitution is no longer grounds for legal action against them, they tend on the whole to keep to their traditional role by refusing to engage in such practices.

Nonetheless the emotive force which radiates from the graceful and stimulating silhouette of the geisha, from her voice and from her slightest gesture has a power over men which originates in the deepest erotic impulses.

Engravings on wood.

1 *(facing)* — The ideograms which form the caption of the drawing describe the moment immediately preceding orgasm, the irresistible rising of the secretions which culminate in ectasy. The two seals are probably those of the painter.

2 *(bottom)* — The woman is a whore; her partner is beginning to doubt the genuineness of the emotion which she has displayed ever since intercourse started. Either he should be proud of it, or she is a clever impostor. To put her to the test, he swears that henceforth he will make love to no other woman. She proclaims her good faith, saying that she could not achieve ecstasy with a man with whom she was not in love.

3 *(top right)* — "Is that really so?" asks the man. "Go even deeper into me yet" replies the woman.

4 *(bottom right)* — Persons teasing each other as they recall the dissipated lives they led when young. (School of Utamaro).

43

On this page, two works of Hokusaï. *Above:* the woman is becoming impatient with the preliminary niceties in which the man is engaged, as she wants a full sexual act. He, on the other hand, is delighted with such dallying as it enables him, by means of the yellow band around his penis, to increase his virility even further!

Below: the ideographs contain a brief description of the faint sound caused by the secretions which herald the approach of the female orgasm. In her embarrassment she begs her lover not to consider her immodest; his caresses, on the contrary, give her the greatest pleasure, and while he is stroking his mistress's organ the man enquires whether she is happy.

Below: the sign explains the painting. Literally it should be translated as "leech" or "cudgel", understood naturally in a sexual sense. (Work of Toyokuni).

The woman intends to extract the fullest pleasure from each minute, as her lover has to leave soon for a long time. The moment of ecstasy is approaching, and with it the secretions which reveal the intensity of her passion are flowing more abundantly, wetting the sheets, while the man is seized by the most supreme pleasure.

47

其ノ貳

Above: the man is proud of his penis. He is about to achieve orgasm, his third for that night, whereas his partner is preparing to enjoy her thirty-third climax and is accordingly full of admiration for the amorous technique of her lover. (Work of Kusinada).

Right: they have been united five times in a supreme orgasm. And yet he wants to enter her once more. Now he observes her, as she writhes in her blissful paroxysm and is visibly impressed by her ardor. She grips the mosquito-net curtains, at the very pinnacle of amorous exaltation. (Toyokuni).

Following pages: the soliloquy of the involuntary Peeping-Tom (left), who watches as the woman he covets is about to be seduced by another. (Kuniyoshi).

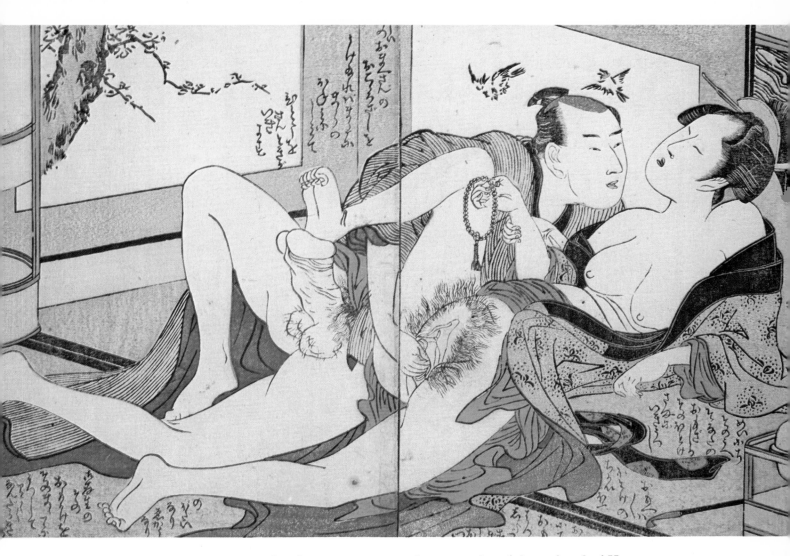

On these two pages, three works of the school of Utamaro.
Top left: the old man with his ear glued to the ground is the husband of the woman who is making love with the young man. Puzzled by the sound made by the movements of his rival's penis in his wife's vagina, he decides that he will bring the question up later. They are talking about him. His wife hates him. Her new lover advises the disconsolate young woman, nonetheless, to make love with the old man five or six times a day until he dies from exhaustion.

Facing: the monologue and poem of the thief. He thinks that the couple is going to fall asleep while still united and then separate during their sleep. Having seen the penis of the other man, he concludes that none of his companions can rival him. Fleetingly the idea occurs to him to tie up the couple in order to seduce the woman, but he eventually decides against it and, instead, writes a poem.

Above: on the anniversary of her husband's death the woman recalls his memory. The man now living with her is quite as good as him; she tells him so and he thanks her for the compliment.

Two lovers trade accusations of infidelity. "Let us go and make love somewhere", says the woman. But the man will have none of it. (Works of Eisen and Utamaro).

"The Samuraï and the bonze each know
The ways of pleasure;
It sometimes happens that
They are on it then together".

"The heart of a woman does not beat only
Under her left breast".

"By the tenderness with which she warms
Between her hands
The bird which has fallen from its nest,
You shall identify the one
who hopes to caress your feather".

Right: the woman wants her companion to fulfil her desires quickly, but only when he has taken shelter under the mosquito net. She is naked, and he is so impatient that he can feel his ejaculation coming even before he enters her.
Bottom: She has caught him taking a nap and admits that, at the sight of his body, she can no longer contain herself. Her husband died three years ago and she cannot manage without sexual pleasure. She need not worry, though, as he will come every day, if necessary, to bring her excitement.

THE GOLDEN AGE OF PLEASURE AND EROTIC ART

Yoshiwara is inseparable from Japanese erotic art. This veritable Mecca of pleasure was the setting for its highest manifestations for more than 250 years, and still is today.

Yoshiwara is the 'floating world', the 'city without night', grafted onto Edo, the future Tokyo, as a result of a political change which occurred early in the 17th century which made that city the new capital of Japan.

Yoshiwara was home to the golden age of erotic painting, and was distinguished by some of the greatest artists—to such an extent that their successors often continued to draw their inspiration from their works. Those masters were Utamaro, Hokusaï, Shunsho, Toyokuni and Eisen, some of whose compositions, as is only fitting, are included in this volume.

In our quest for the best sources to illustrate the prodigious pictorial adventure which took place in Yoshiwara we found that choosing from among such an abundance of riches was no easy matter. In actual fact the role of Yoshiwara in the history of Japan was not entirely passive: this secret capital of sex was, in the last century, the seedbed of a coup d'état which put an end to a positively medieval type of feudal régime which existed in Japan at the same time as the conquest of the American West and the first European industrial revolution.

YOSHIWARA, A GARDEN OF DELIGHTS

If the most powerful kings and princes of Europe once lived in the midst of large and brilliant courts, they did so less in order to make them centers of art, culture and pleasure than to keep a closer watch on their followers.

For similar reasons, in 1603, Edo—the modern Tokyo—became the capital of Japan, according to the wishes of the Shogun Ieyasu. After him the Tokugawa clan, of which he was a member, was to govern the country until 1867, keeping it under a feudal régime until the last century. The shogun, whose title means Generalissimo, was nothing less than a dictator; the power of the emperor, who lived 300 miles away in Kyoto, being reduced to the purely spiritual.

This historical preamble is important because, as a by-product of the politics of the rule of the shoguns, it brought into being the Plain of Reeds, or Yoshiwara, Tokyo's pleasure district.

One of the first decisions of Shogun Ieyasu was to compel his vassals, the *daymio,* to leave their provinces and live, in many cases, for more than one year out of two, in Edo. By forcing them, moreover, to leave their families as hostages in the capital when they had to spend time in their home areas, the sovereign curbed any temptation they might have had to plot against him. The journeys which this arrangement involved, however, were very long. The 300-mile road along which they traveled was soon bordered with relay stations

"If she sucks the grains of rice
Of which your saké is made
It will only be the better for it".

"Sowing seeds is nothing, if
One neglects
one's garden thereafter".

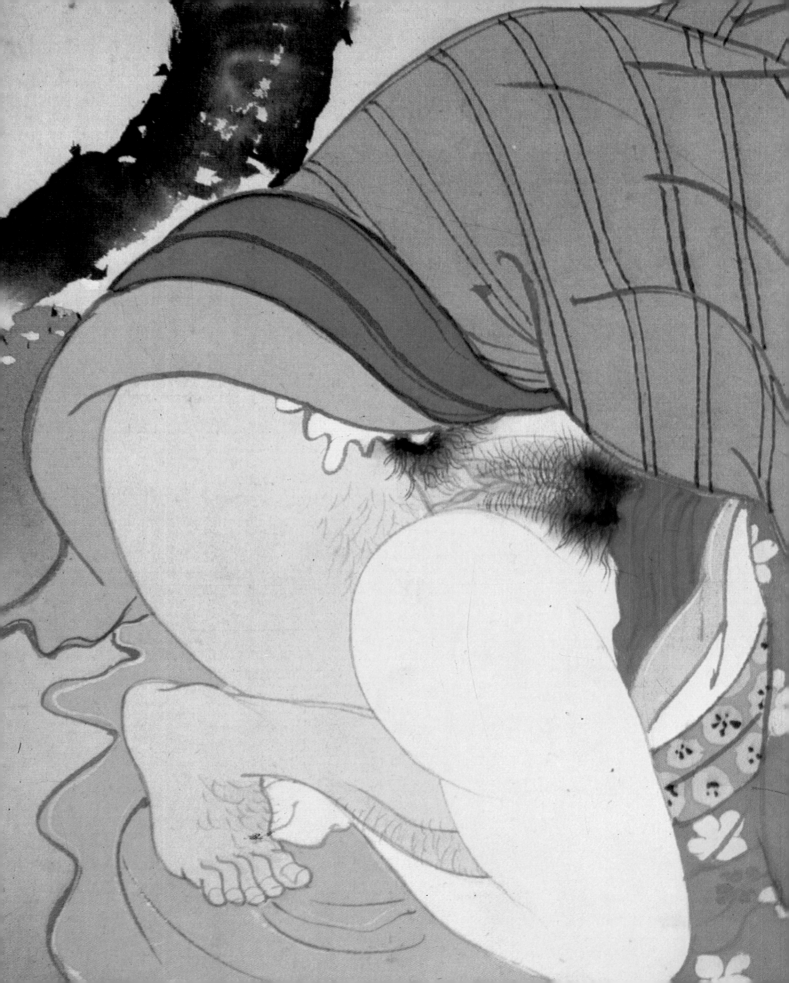

"In the midst of the thickest forest,
Desire always finds a place for the tree of life".

"The difference between war and love
Lies in the nature of the target
Offered to the lance of the Samuraï".

Preceding pages, above and right: Specimens of original paintings on silk describing twelve months of sexual relations, presented in the form of a fold-out.

A peasant raping a girl *(preceding pages)*. — A *moxa* doctor making love to one of his patients, a geisha. (*Moxa* is a form of medicine not unlike acupuncture, in which pinpricks are replaced by contact with burning material). — While his mother is with a neighbor, the child strikes him with a toy sword.

which soon became friendly inns, where attentive serving-wenches did their utmost to help the lonely gentlemen who stopped there at night to forget the strains of their journey. Many of them went further, accompanying their transient lovers as far as their next night's halt. Some of them, driven by ambition and money, thus came to follow them all the way to the capital, where they settled. A large number of these girls were young peasants from the small town of Moto Yoshiwara, in the province of Tokaido. This was how Tokyo's red light district acquired its name. Although it was closed three and half centuries later in 1957, on the orders of the present emperor, it is still a synonym for prostitute or, at the very least, for woman of easy virtue.

Yoshiwara grew until it had become, by the middle of the 17th century, a town within a town. It even had its own gates, which were closed each evening, though that did not necessarily mean that the clients of the courtesans went back home. Utamaro, one of the masters of the erotic print of the *ukiyo-é,* or 'floating world', lived there for almost half of his life.

Yoshiwara really did provide artists with a virtually inexhaustible source of inspiration,

"Take me in your arms, said the woman.
The man took her. And remained, for the rest of his life,
Between her hands".

"Learn how to measure the hilt of your sabre
When you slip it into the sheath of a virgin".

"If his penis reaches down to the ground,
Maybe it is less thick than long".

"Woman does not have a thousand mouths.
But all of hers Attract kisses".

On these two pages and page 70, reproductions of works attributed to Kunisada or his disciples, from the end of the 18th or beginning of the 19th centuries. They were one of the bedside books of the aristocracy.

Left: The woman is saying: "Not now, my baby is going to wake up". He could not care less, as he wants to take her right away. As for his own baby (his penis), it is already well awake.

Right: She urges him to make love, but he talks about aphrodisiac potions and contraceptives.

and businessmen with the promise of quick riches. This was because an opulent city sprang up around the Green Houses where the courtesans held sway—a kind of free trade zone where anything could be sold. Craftsmen opened up shops; studios working with precious metals and jewelry, tea houses, hotels and restaurants increased in number. A parallel society was organized, borrowing its structures from the outside world on the basis of social class and the incomes which individuals could afford to devote to pleasure. The less-well-off had to make do with the services of 'rubbers of legs' or 'lotus leaves' who provided massage for the clients of the bathing establishments and second-rate inns, whereas the Green Houses were reserved for the elite of the courtesans who lived there surrounded by young apprentices. Lovemaking went on day and night, of course, but the girls also talked about literature, while a renowned painter worked on a portrait of the lady of the house or of her best-endowed followers. In their chambers, which were decorated with costly and rare objects, the *oiran* (courtesans) at the top of the scale lived sumptuously off the generosity of merchants who had to travel regularly to Edo on business. The Samuraï or soldiers of fortune, preferred the company of young boys; this was also true of the bonzes,

Facing: The lover is the woman's adopted son, now a widow. She had been afraid that he might be impotent; however, she has been re-assured and wants him to forget that she is, in the eyes of the law, his mother, and satisfy her craving. Unless he gives her the fullest possible pleasure she will never allow him to marry.

Bottom: It is not the size of a clitoris that is important but its ability to cause orgasm, the man explains to his partner, and the same is true of a penis. Whereupon he assures her that, since she is merely a concubine and not a wife, she should not feel remorse about deceiving her master. And she really does not care: all she wants is pleasure from him.

who, although Yoshiwara was out of bounds to them—on pain of death—did venture in there from time to time in disguise, looking for nice young male companions.

Dance performances were presented by the *odoriko,* or dancing girls, who regardless of their rank in the complex hierarchy of the Plain of Reeds, were organized, like the singing girls *(geiko),* in guilds which were quite separate from those of the prostitutes. Rather than Plain of Reeds, most of the faithful used their own code expression, the Plain of Joy.

Erotic literature was clearly not absent from Fulayo (City without Night), where writers, publishers and booksellers all flocked in search of glory, since it was easier to acquire at Yoshiwara than in the austere palace of the shogun and his court, even though according to custom he lived there surrounded by large numbers of concubines.

Just as Edo had its own pleasure district, Kyoto, with Shimbara, and Osaka, with Shimmachi, also had theirs. Like Yoshiwara, they owed much of their prosperity to the fact that the shogun used to send the *daymio* on mission to the major provincial towns when they had won his confidence by promoting his cause at court. In this way, far from the capital and even back in their own provinces, they still found this 'floating world' which the distrust of the first of the Tokugawa had helped bring into being for the sake of political stability. Much later, Yoshiwara was to lead to their downfall. It was in the privacy of its Green Houses, safely tucked away behind the town's iron gates which were closed at midnight, that the apparently devoted vassals of the shogun plotted a revolution which brought about the downfall, in 1867, of a power structure 264 years old and opened the Enlightened or Meiji Period in Japanese history.

*"The stall of a merchant of spring
Is closed only once in a moon".*

In the boat: They are playing with words, exploring the associations between their names and the art of love-making. The woman's name seems to mean something like 'wooden pestle', and they make two three puns on this theme.

Right page: Sexually frustrated males are compared to cats whose dinner consists solely of a dried-up fish. (Engraving on wood, in color, about 1870).

"There are some tomcats who prefer
Female cats with short hair".

"A bonze will fornicate just as he drinks:
Too much, but without regard
For the fragility of the bottle".

"*Fear the venom of the moon fish*
Only when the river is red".

"*The whore who dresses up like a nun*
Honors more than the gods".

Left: Lesbians and group scene, two prints by Harunobu.

Above: A concubine to whom an old man is boasting of his virility while at the same time admitting that his penis is no bigger than that of a child. Twenty years earlier he could satisfy a woman fifteen or twenty times a night without fail. Now he has fallen far short of such standards. He is, however, determined to prove his sexual power once again, and despite his partner's objections he succeeds.

Above: his wife having evaded his amorous onslaught, the persistent husband rapes her.

Top right: The man with the long pipe is blind. His wife takes advantage of the fact in order to have intercourse with her lover. But the cuckold is intrigued by the noise of their passionate writhing, and the unfaithful wife, out of fear, promptly stops.

Bottom: the intervention of his wife, who grabs him by the hair, prevents the husband from making love yet again to his step-daughter, who is lying naked by his side. He had invited her into his house ostensibly as a maid. The young girl promptly claims that she she has been seduced against her will.

*"Only he who puts on
The jade chignon of a geisha
can tell what joys it hides".*

*"Choose the she-wolf rather than the bitch,
She is wilder but more faithful".*

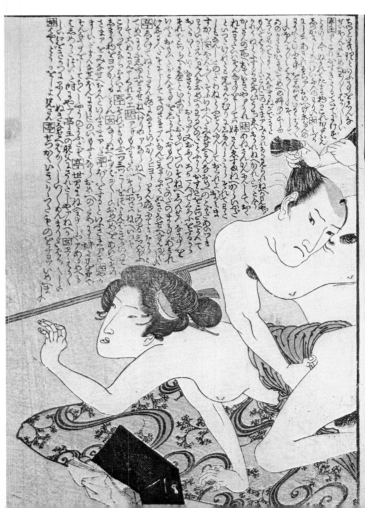
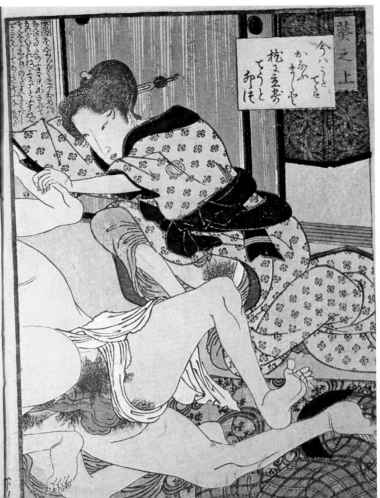

"*The virgin excites the ardor of your penis,*
The geisha gives it a little wit
And much wisdom".

"*If you know how to approach her*
She will mix every night
Her honey with your milk".

"*If you plant your knife*
In a tuft of spring grass,
Push it in as far as the root".

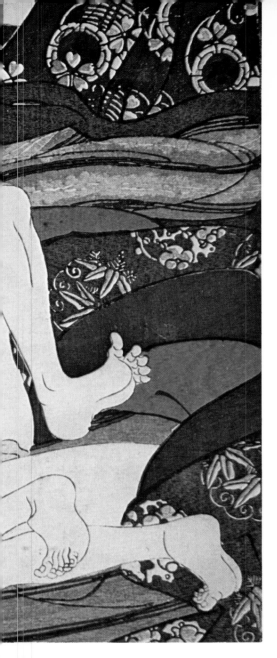

"On board the floating world of pleasures
The good sailor does not dream of going ashore again".

"A chimney which is still warm
Does not fear the visit of the chimney-sweep".

"He who loves can hold
A flower in each hand".

"There are some flowers which bloom
Better by moonlight than in the sun".

Two illustrations from *Komoncho*, a title which one American scholar has rendered as *Notebook of Small Drawings*, while the Institute for Sex Research of the University of Indiana translates it as *The Small Bed Curtain*.

Right: Their passion is completely spent, as can be seen from the scattered sheets and crumpled papers. The girl, sated with pleasure, her eyes half-closed and with a languid smile on her lips, is stretched out, while her lover leans under the mosquito net to fill a cup of tea. In *Japanese Erotic Art*, Richard Illing finds in this work a splendid expression of the plenitude of physical happiness which prolongs the mutual pleasure produced by a perfect harmony between the sexes.

*"If you do not know why he loves you,
his penis will tell you.
If you do not know why you love him,
It will tell you that too".*

*"Sooner the moist and warm leather
Of a good harigata, than the penis
of a blunderer".*

THE SCHOOL OF THE COURTESANS

Prostitution prospered in the Japan of the *ukiyo-é,* or Floating World. Yet this ephemeral place where an unending feast of sensual delights made the dreams of many come true, was actually governed by a strictly hierarchical organization.

Erotic prints, through their studied exaggeration of sex organs, may well express a pathological hedonism utterly lacking in romanticism, but the conduct of the courtesans followed a set of conventions which in their own way were quite as rigorous as those of the imperial court. And in fact the *oirans*—the name for the occupants of the Green Houses— were given virtually the same kind of education as the geishas; only its purpose was different.

From the age of seven the future prostitute learned singing and music and was initiated into the complex rites of the tea ceremony, under the strict supervision of the experienced ladies of the establishment where she would later put her charms to professional use. One of them would take her under her protection, becoming both her Elder Sister (her actual title) and moral tutor, as it were. At the age of twelve the young girl acceded to the status of *kamouro,* the culmination of the first five years of apprenticeship. Next came three years of further studies. The would-be *oiran* was allowed to watch the amorous technique of her tutor through the cracks in the blinds of the partitions or even more directly through the half-open—indeed, never closed—door of the bedroom. This kind of clinical voyeurism

Left: plate from the *Vagaries of Love,* one of the parts of *Haru-Akebono* (The Beginning of Spring), a bedside book from the 17th or 18th centuries.

Below: plate from Tsumagasane *(Sleeping Side by Side);* the proprietor of a brothel marries one of his employees. The husband is aged twenty, and his wife sixteen. However, due to over-indulgence in sex he dies at the age of twenty-three. His wife is so deeply saddened that she retires to a peaceful cottage, to spend her days reciting the *Neubutsu,* as a tribute to the dead. Time passes, however, and desire returns to her loins. After all, she is only eighteen. She therefore asks her maid, in the utmost secrecy, to find her a suitable lover.

Right page, two new episodes from Tsumagasane:

1. The maid brings her mistress a man renowned for the remarkable size of his sexual organ. The young woman is, however, greatly disappointed, having been deceived by appearances; she rebukes the go-between, who promises to redeem herself promptly.

2. This time the maid has chosen a candidate whom her mistress has already noticed at the public baths and with whom she has since fallen in love. With him she soon reaches an orgasm. Listening for the resonant echoes of their pleasure, the maid herself becomes excited. As it happens, the man with the enormous penis then appears on the scene; she pounces on him and compels him to make love. Both of them are fully satisfied.

enabled her to acquaint herself quickly with the attitudes of men and the proper ways to respond. When she reached the age of fifteen she herself was authorized to put these lessons into practice.

The young girl, who though still a beginner was clearly very knowledgeable, was then promoted to the rank of *shinzo.* She then started her quest for a protector, whose sensual attachment to her, once confirmed by the frequency of his visits and gifts, would truly mark her accession to the status or *oiran.* This rank would qualify her for a room of her own, as well as the company of two *shinzo* who served her in return for the training which she dispensed to them. If, however, she was unfortunate enough to fail to persuade one of her clients to sponsor her, she had to remain content with the title of *hippon,* while waiting for a chance to become an *oiran* by virtue of seniority. Such failures could be costly: as Lesoualc'h points out, she would be required to pay out of her own pocket for the lavish celebrations of the *shinzo dashi,* the ceremony which took place in honor of a girl's first steps in the profession.

At this precise moment the independence of the young *oiran* hung in the balance. Having failed to secure the support of a faithful and generous lover at the outset of her career, she was obliged to get into debt. And, curiously enough, lovers *were* faithful, as the rules forbade the same man to visit two occupants of the same house successively.

Competition was fierce, as can be seen from 17th-century figures which classify the courtesans by social standing. At the bottom of the scale were the *jororu;* these low-grade houses where prostitutes used to call numbered about three thousand in Yoshiwara, whereas there were only three *tayu,* the most élite of the rich and famous courtesans. Between these two extremes there were about two thousand women, belonging to four categories: *koshi,* immediately below the *tayu,* and then *tsubone, hamacha* and *jijoro.*

The most famous of the courtesans led lives of splendor and luxury, coupled with great influence even beyond the walls of the city of pleasure. They were indulged in everything, and their whims had the force of law. However, they did have to abide scrupulously by certain conventions, for example, by sustaining a quasi-literary correspondence with their lovers.

With age, the others became the pariahs of this parallel society. Like the heroine of Ihara Saikaku they resembled in name only the Merchants of Spring whom they so envied as girls. Steadily declining over the years, they wandered throughout the country, moving out of the towns so as to stand a better chance of seducing the more credulous provincials. They went from sex-starved tramp to grasping and perverted bonze; or they might join one of those boats, whose crew of prostitutes—known as the singing bonzesses—steered their way, to the sound of music, amongst the filth which littered the river near the sea. In order

These scenes of simple tenderness are restful and re-assuring, in the midst of the delirium of passion. (*a*/ painting attributed to Hokuba, early 19th century; *b*/ painting by Schunchô, 18th century).

Right: Extracts from a work which was without any doubt a bedside book in the 19th century.

*"Between the island of the Amazons and that of the ephebes
There is only a narrow stretch of sea".*

*"Solitary pleasure is a silent woman
Who never says no".*

to attract attention they used a kind of castanet, the *yotsu take,* as an accompaniment. The luckiest of them became salesgirls in various businesses, including fabrics, where buyers were entitled to relish their favors, once the purchase was complete. The daughter of carnal lust whose adventures were related by Saikaku even became a public scribe specializing in the writing of love letters; a *koshimoto,* or lady-in-waiting to a woman of noble rank; then she worked for a broker in Osaka whose business was always prospering, judging by the perpetual "dampness of his writing table". Actually the income which he recorded on his tablets came for the most part from prostitution by his staff.

However, there was one common feature shared by the capitals of sensuality and the shabby establishments at the bottom of the scale: the cult of a peculiarly Japanese erotism, the quality of which has suffered less than elsewhere as a result of promiscuity. This is doubtless because sexual pleasure in all its forms, even considered as an end in itself, and a notion of law which was quite undisturbed by morality, continued to generate an art which was closely linked to the country's cultural heritage. In this way, while the masters of the *ukiyo-é* made portraits of the leading courtesans, guides recruited from among eminent and respectable men of letters set their calligraphy aside as soon as night fell, in order to inform visitors of the rates currently being charged in the different houses of pleasure.

*"Knowledgeable gardeners always begin
By watering the spring grass".*

*"Everything can be done with lip service,
Even love".*

*"Woman is a shamisen;
Learn to make her three strings vibrate
And she will enjoy your music".*

*"The warrior who has lost
The use of his two hands
Still has an eleventh finger left".*

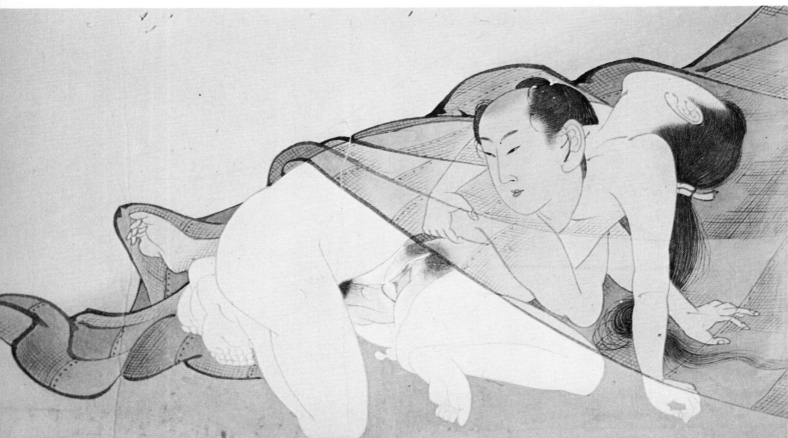